TAKING YOUR LIFE TO NEW HEIGHTS

by

MAX GOLD

 World Publishing and Productions

Planestorming!

Published by World Publishing & Productions P.O. Box 8722 Jupiter, FL 33468; worldpublishingandproductions.com

ISBN: 978-1-957111-15-5

Library of Congress Control Number: 2023907138

For Christine, Jonathan, & Maxine

Table of Contents

Planestorming!

Thank you!

This will be challenging. I am sorry if I didn't thank you—I promise I appreciate everyone who has helped me get to this point in life.

First, to my "dads": Thank you to my Heavenly Father, who has guided and covered me and my family throughout the trials of life. Next, to my spiritual father, Bishop Kelvin L. Cobaris, who spent the last 15+ years helping and teaching my family how to live and love as Christ did. Next, to my biological father, Robert Gold, who showed me how to work hard and has been my biggest supporter and ear in life, especially as I ventured off to build a business. Love you, Pops! A special thank you to my Band of Brother, Guy Shashaty. You take my wounded heart and fill it up every year at the Boot Camps. Love you, Brother. Next, to my business father Chris Koob, who patiently taught me a system on leadership development in the business world. Thank you, Coach!

Next to my family: To my grandparents—may you all rest in peace. I have such fond memories of all of you and love you forever. To Maxine and Jonathan—I love you both so much. I am so sorry we lost Mom. I am so sorry for the many mistakes that I made as a parent. I pray for you daily and that you forgive me. I will try my absolute best to be there for you in the way that you need me as your dad. God Bless you both. To my mom, who I love dearly. Thank you for always checking in on me and for your love and care, and especially for what you do for the grandbabies! To my siblings, Gaby, Lily, Ben, Matt, and Melissa—I love and miss you all! To Sheri and Ted—thank you for being great parents, too, over the years! I love you. To Lyz—thank you for coming into my life. GBU & love you. I pray for you (& Lily) each and every day. To my 49 crew and Pier! 1love. See you every 5 years! To my business associates—I love you all. Extra love to the Koob, Henry, Farmer, Hobbs, and Greer families. What you did, especially when we lost the matriarch of the family will never be forgotten. To Don Ienner—thank you for hiring me in 1996. I literally went from music industry rags to riches overnight when you gave me a shot at Columbia/Sony. You taught me how to be fearless in business. To my first coaches, Rett & Pat Summerville—you opened an office and changed my life when I walked in it in 2004. Thank you. To our editorial staff, Julie & Kimberly—you are angels from heaven. Thank you. This would not have happened without you. To our wonderful team and Goldrush Hierarchy—I love you and am proud of all of you. Extra thank you to Brandon & Latrice Smith for your patience, hard work, and loyalty. To my clients in the airline industry—I thank you and love you from the bottom of my heart. Planestorming was entirely written while I traveled from base to base to sit with you all. To all my colleagues and "friends of Bill" in the program who have helped me obtain sobriety for 25+ years (God willing)—thank you for always having a place for me to go. To Christine's family—I love you all and pray for peace and continued love in your hearts. To my Band of Brothers around the country—coin up! I love you guys. Once again, thank you all. My heart is full of joy. Even in the darkest of times, I have peace.

Psalm 23

Joshua 24:15

Introduction

D o you remember the first time you were on a plane and looked out the window? You probably did not have the spiritual insight you may possess now, but something inside may have made you wonder, *Where does this world come from?*

As the plane began to taxi and you peered out of the thick little odd-shaped window, your view of the world changed. Then you became increasingly mesmerized as the plane lifted into the air and the cars faded away. The plane elevated higher, and the buildings seemed to shrink. Within just a few short minutes, you could make out every landmark.

My first memories of flying were from trips I took with my family during spring break. My dad would board my sister Gaby and me on a plane from LaGuardia airport for a journey to Ft. Lauderdale, Florida, to see my loving Grandma Blanche and tough but kind Grandpa Murray.

"Look - Central Park, the World Trade Center, the Statue of Liberty." I would stare in disbelief, trying to comprehend how we could be flying like an eagle 30,000 feet above the ground. We took many of those trips back and forth to Florida, but if this book were to start there, it might become a series. So it's time to get back on track!

Let me give you the cliff notes on how the rest of my life has gone. After I graduated from college, I moved back to New York City, where I pursued the music industry for ten years, doing well. Then I met my dream girl and her son. After I got laid off from a great job, I went through a period of depression as I dealt with being just over broke and all the turmoil and introspection that came with being in NYC during 9/11. Then my girl and I got married, I adopted her two-year-old son, and we moved to Orlando, Florida. There I started a business, she built a large hairstyling client base, and we had our daughter. Although life was full of the usual ups and downs, we grew spiritually, based our marriage on love, and lived our lives keeping our priorities in what we believe is the correct order: God, family, then business. Although there were cloudy days, the sun shined a lot.

Throughout our travels, we took many airplanes, and I was able to look out of those windows—sometimes crystallized from the wintry altitudes. Our middle-income family of four (five with our Shih Tzu, Bam Bam) was enjoying life.

Then, on April 9, 2018, my life changed forever.

The absolute love of my life, Christine, suffered an unexpected stroke.

We spent 11 incredibly long days in the hospital—including our wedding anniversary. Then, on April 19, my Queen was gone. She passed from a procedure that didn't blend well with her brain.

Okay, so I just dropped a bomb on you. "Max, this isn't supposed to be a tearjerker." Sorry about that! I just needed to set the tone for you so you can understand my heart. I'm a pretty positive guy, so I promise it will be fun and challenging from here on in.

"Okay, so where do we go now?" you might be asking.

Well, the world has become a place where we don't have a millisecond to think for ourselves. Our 17 social media sites send us countless alerts. Text messages come in like we are running a global newswire. And our phones ring all day long like a broken cathedral bell.

I want to invite you to Planestorm!

Whether you are on a shuttle from JFK to DC, a cross-country flight from NWK to LAX, a Key West puddle jumper, or a red-eye from San Fran to Tokyo, this is YOUR time to change your life.

If you are reading this and are on your flight, please follow these simple steps:

Put that phone on airplane mode.

Planestorming!

Turn the dimness all the way down on that TV in front of you.

Turn off your Bluetooth headphones.

Grab a cup of coffee.

And strap on your seat belt!

It's time to get to work. Together, we will lay out your flight plan so you can make the rest of your life the BEST of your life!

I wouldn't call this a book; it's more of a guide. Together, we will address the many areas of life and formulate your plan for breakthrough!

Are you ready? Did you do the things I asked you?

Sweeeet! Let's go on a journey!

Throughout each chapter, I'm going to ask you to do some heartwork. Sometimes it will be maintenance; at other times, parts of your plane may need an upgrade. As we taxi down the runway, I'd like you to grab a pen, consider the following questions, and write down some thoughtful answers.

Who is important in your life?

_____

_____

_____

_____

What would you deem are the most important activities in your life?

_____

_____

_____

_____

Planestorming!

What takes precedence in your day?

_____

_____

_____

_____

_____

Are those things that take precedence the most important parts of your life?

_____

_____

_____

_____

_____

How do you make time for God to talk to you?

_____

_____

_____

_____

_____

"And the house which king Solomon built for the LORD, the length thereof was threescore cubits, and the breadth thereof twenty cubits, and the height thereof thirty cubits. And the porch before the temple of the house, twenty cubits was the length thereof, according to the breadth of the house; and ten cubits was the breadth thereof before the house."

1 Kings 6:2-3 KJV

Planestorming!

Lose Your Baggage

It's okay to walk away from damaged luggage.

Did you ever stand around waiting at the carousel, wondering why everyone else has claimed their luggage and yours is still nowhere in sight? You double-check the marquis, making sure you are at the right numbered area.

"Maybe this is for another flight," you say to yourself, and then you watch the guy who was in your neighboring seat grab his valise and go off into the sunset. At some point, you feel defeated and inquire about where to report the lost luggage.

When you walk into the tiny room flooded with orphan bags, you feel like a complete loser. My clothes, my toiletries, my security of home away from home are all lost or missing. You fill out a form and make a pledge to answer every incoming call that afternoon, waiting for your airline to call with some good news.

Planestorming!

This is what we do in life.

We hang on desperately, hoping that meaningless stuff can return to us and stay in our possession. Sometimes we try to regain something good, like a childhood memory or a happy relationship we've lost. Other times, we simply can't let go of the pain—perhaps from a poor financial decision or the fall-out of the time you got too drunk at the company party. These memories can sit and stew in your mind for days, months, or even years, becoming added weight, which in turn becomes excess baggage.

You know what?

Until you intentionally lose your luggage, you will remain stuck in the wilderness.

I know—from personal experience. For years, I held onto the pain and sorrow from my past. I let my wounded heart take control of my life as I attended my own long-drawn-out pity party.

Whether you are 18 or 88, I challenge you to be okay with losing your bags. It's not going to be easy. It is going to take work. For that 18-year-old, your luggage may cling to you, slowing you down until you're 28 or older. And if you are the 88-year-old, you better hurry up and let it go!

"You mean there is not a quick fix for this?"

No, but there is a solution and a remedy.

"What steps can I take to deal with this?" you ask.

Well, first, you need to be brutally honest with yourself. Haha! That's not too easy. Most of the time, we let ourselves off the hook with that.

So here's a better suggestion: take the most important person in your life (other than your 2-year-old, lol) out to lunch or dinner and ask them what they think of you. Ask them what areas they think you need to change. So basically, you are paying for someone to slap you in the face! Ouch! I promise if you do this and stay quiet while they're talking, it will sting at first, but you will be provided with the ammo to look within and make the necessary adjustments.

At the end of this chapter are some questions you can ask that chosen one. This is not an easy exercise. Here's a warning: You may be tempted to go from friend to friend and family member to family member, attempting to find that one person who will tell you you're perfect.

Don't do it!

Planestorming!

My dad does this when he has a sports injury or mild illness. He's been a die-hard basketball player for 60+ years, and when he gets hurt, he goes from doctor to doctor until he gets the all-clear!

My suggestion is that you go to that one person who means everything to you, buy them that bacon cheeseburger, Nicoise salad, or pastrami sandwich, lather the metaphorical Vaseline on your face, and tell them to let you have it! Swallow your pride for an hour, sit on your hands, keep your mouth stuffed with food, and hang in there! This will not take too much time, but it's the icebreaker for changing your life! Once that's done, you get to move on to the present-day you!

Need more help with this? Look below for an idea of the questions you can ask them. Feel free to use the blank space in this book to jot down their responses, and don't be afraid to let the conversation develop beyond these questions. Remember, in order to grow, you must be proactive. Alright, you have seven days to complete this task.

Ready, go!

ON YOUR OWN:

Brainstorm who your go-to person is. Who can you trust to be brutally honest with you?

_____

_____

_____

_____

What's your flight plan? When will you take off and navigate your course? Make sure you set a specific time to meet with your flight attendant.

_____

_____

_____

_____

Planestorming!

Strategize your take-off. This won't be an easy conversation to begin. How can you set the scene to chart your course?

_____

_____

_____

_____

_____

TAKE OFF ON YOUR JOURNEY:

Include these questions, but don't be afraid to come up with your own. Feel free to take this book to take notes, or, if it's more comfortable, record their answers as soon as you land from your mission—but make sure to do so before the engines cool!

QUESTIONS TO GUIDE YOUR FUTURE ROUTE

Tell me about the areas where you think I need to improve?

_____

_____

_____

_____

_____

_____

_____

_____

What are my flaws, in your opinion?

_____

_____

_____

_____

_____

_____

_____

_____

_____

_____

_____

What observations of me do you have regarding my personality, and what should I change or work on? Shoot straight, what baggage do I need to lose?

_____

_____

_____

_____

_____

_____

_____

_____

_____

_____

_____

OTHER QUESTIONS TO ASK OR OBSERVATIONS YOU MADE:

_____

_____

_____

_____

_____

_____

_____

_____

_____

_____

_____

Max Gold

Planestorming!

"B" or "E" - The Middle Seat

A self-assessment of your present situation.

Why the middle seat as a chapter title? Well, I don't know about you, but that is my least favorite place to sit on a plane. From the middle seat, you can't quite see out of the window. And forget about stretching your legs. When sandwiched between two other bodies, it's tempting to think what it would be like to sit in the aisle seat. Man, it would be so nice to pop in and out to the restroom!

But despite the inconvenience, the middle seat is your present situation.

I assume you are reading this book because you want a more prestigious seat in life. If you did the assessment in the previous chapter, you probably either feel beat up or inspired. Either way, that is okay! Now we need to build upon that conversation and start to evaluate where we are so we can figure out where we want to go.

For me, there was a period of about four to five years after the Great Recession when I simply existed. At the time, our son Jonathan was a teenager, and our daughter Maxine was a toddler. I was in my 30s, and man, life was moving like molasses. My income was low, we were living to pay bills, and it seemed like I wanted to wave the white surrender flag every day. But worse than my situation was my mindset—and I didn't realize that until much later! I was living my life in a complete blur, just going through the motions. I wasn't even counting down the days to Friday night because I was working on Saturdays, too.

My 30s were rough. I'm not saying this has to be the age range when this happens; it most certainly can affect anyone. However, that was a difficult time for me. My kids were at tough ages, and though I love them more than anything, I wouldn't want to relive that period of their lives!

Eventually, I got out of that funk, and while I'm grateful, I regret that it took me so long. I sat in my own mess for years because I didn't have the tools to move forward. Sound familiar?

If you recognize you may be wasting years, but can't quite pinpoint the direction you need to take, perhaps it's time to open your eyes. Perhaps you are in denial that you have the ability to choose your own seat. So how do you get there? Let's get out that toolbox and stop going through life on autopilot.

The first step is to become fully aware of how you feel. Recognizing where you are is a process that can take a while to evolve. It's time to get in tune with your feelings.

PONDER THE FOLLOWING QUESTIONS THAT MAY APPLY TO YOUR LIFE AND JOURNAL YOUR THOUGHTS.

What do you look forward to most at the start of each day? What gets you out of bed?

_____

_____

_____

_____

_____

How do you fuel yourself in preparation for the events of your day?

_____

_____

_____

_____

_____

What worries consume your mind that threaten to take you off course?

_____

_____

_____

_____

_____

Are you satisfied with where you are in your career?

_____

_____

_____

_____

_____

Do you feel like your relationships are crosschecked or are you flying solo?

_____

_____

_____

_____

_____

LET'S GO DEEPER!

Are there warning signs in your marriage that need attention?

_____

_____

_____

_____

_____

What SOS signs in your other relationships might you be overlooking?

_____

_____

_____

_____

_____

Do you spend adequate time with your kids, parents, and friends?

_____

_____

_____

_____

_____

Is isolating yourself from others becoming a pattern?

_____

_____

_____

_____

_____

Honestly evaluate your recent social media posts. Are you posting that your life is incredible, only to feel like the ultimate loser after closing the app?

_____

_____

_____

_____

_____

_____

What vices are you turning to as a source of medication? (Perhaps alcohol, drugs, or social media?)

_____

_____

_____

_____

_____

Do you lose focus when the going gets tough and neglect to heed the warnings from your instrument panel?

_____

_____

_____

_____

_____

How did you feel about your answers?

_____

_____

_____

_____

_____

_____

Planestorming!

Wherever you are and whatever is revealing itself, don't beat yourself up over the reality of these issues, but at the same time, don't let yourself off the hook. The processing you do now will pave the runway for a stellar takeoff.

But perhaps your new insights have illuminated that it's time to make a change! That's a good place to be! Let's chart a course to mold you into who you want to become tomorrow.

Oh…one more question for you to consider:

If the next five years of your life are like the last, will you be happy?

_____

_____

_____

_____

If your answer to that last question was a simple "yes," great! But chances are, you are now seeing the need for a change in at least one area. Regardless of your answer, we are not called to be stagnant. A plane that stops flying will soon crash to the ground.

It's time to wake up, smell the coffee coming down the aisleway—courtesy of the flight attendant, of course—and get moving!

"I'm inspired, Max," you might say, planning to make a change tomorrow.

You won't. The deadline is right now! ***Make a list below of all toxic things you want to remove from your daily lifestyle.*** It could be that box of candy you dip into every night, the 12 beers you drink to reward you for the "hard day," or the binge-watching of a show you won't care a hoot about next year.

So, go ahead, make the list!

- _____

- _____

- _____

- _____

- _____

- _____

Now read your list aloud! (Did you? You can't read it aloud if you didn't even write it! Go ahead….I'll wait.)

Planestorming!

So now you have an idea of what you want to remove from your life.

Do you remember the person from the first exercise? The one you trusted? I want you to find them again. We often hear the term "accountability partner," which is really just someone who holds us to the flight plan of growth we are undertaking! Who would be better for this role than the person you've already decided to trust?

So go to that person and read them your list—you've already had practice reading it aloud! Together, decide which of those toxic things you want to throw out the exit door first.

"Can't I skip this and plan my landing?" you might be asking.

No! Not until your heart gets healed. You can't achieve your goals without a clear landing strip.

"Don't I have to have a spiritual encounter in order for this to take place?"

I'm glad you asked. My answer would be yes!

The navigation plan is through prayer. You are going to need to pray, and pray, and pray some more. All the way through the miles of this journey. Pray until you are convicted of each vice, asking God which you should tackle first. And then pray as you dump that cargo! And then pray some more when it's gone, making sure that it doesn't get caught in the wind and fly back in your face. And, oh yeah, get that partner to pray with you!

Yes, it's going to take that much prayer to change for the better. But it will all be worth it! Let's start with praying right now....

Dear Most Holy God,

I know I have baggage I need to dump. Thank you for showing me my shortcomings and where I am messing up. Give me the wisdom to know how to tackle each vice and the courage and strength to rid myself of them. Thank you for the accountability partner you have already prepared for me. Mesh our schedules and help me be transparent with them and with myself. God, I want to be all you are calling me to be! Thank you for giving me this opportunity to refine my patterns so that I can go where you want me to go. In Jesus' name, I pray.

Amen.

I can promise you two things: God hears you and you will see a shift in your life as you go through this process.

Remember, to achieve a successful ascension, you need to complete these steps intentionally—this is as important as reading a flight manual. It can be tempting to tell yourself that you will go back and complete these tasks later, but we are human, and procrastination can turn to a lifetime of inaction. The sooner you tackle this, the sooner you will have results!

Or do you think you are doing so well that these basic maneuvers don't apply to you? Don't let the devil fool you! We are all a work in progress, which means we all have work to do until we get to heaven!

If you are feeling really adventurous, here are a few additional topics to ponder. (WARNING: Proceeding beyond the basic may take you to a higher elevation!)

List three things I want to remove my daily life in order of urgency.

1._____

2._____

3._____

Now dream a little bit. Imagine things a year from today. How will removing this extra weight enrich and make a difference in your life?

_____

_____

_____

First Class

Living the life you deserve.

"Welcome to your flight. We will now begin boarding our first-class passengers."

How many times have you heard that while waiting at your gate? That announcement is usually the 10-minute warning for my turn to board the plane! Why is that? Why don't we deserve to be in the front?

Whenever I get on my flight, I briefly eyeball all the people sitting in first class on my way to the common person's land. Lol. I always wonder what the folks who sit up front do for a living. Are they athletes, heirs to royalty, million milers, kids born with silver spoons in their mouths? Who cares! I just want to get up there on a regular basis.

Before writing this book, I sat in those coveted luxury seats just twice in my life! Please don't assume prestige is the biggest perk of being in first class. That may be why many people like it, but for me, it's about convenience, comfort, and tranquility. Let's face it:

- First-class passengers board prior to all others.

- Their seats are more comfortable and spacious.

- The cabin service is extraordinary.

But, despite these frills, the truth is that first-class passengers are no different than you and me!

So what qualifies us to fly first class?

By this, of course, I am not referring to actually flying first class. (However, if the changes you implement lead to a financial increase, you may often find yourself reclining in the posh seats!) No, I'm talking about living the "first-class life," the life that, for some reason, most people never attain.

The world is full of complacent settlers who allow their past or present circumstances to set them back or keep them frozen, preventing them from living the life they deserve.

Hopefully, you have hit the point where you are truly ready to be proactive and make the necessary changes to clear the runway, making a path so you can finally work for what you deserve. Yes, I said WORK! If you don't do the work, you won't get the results.

For now, let's just focus on the pre-work: Affirmations.

The way you talk to yourself has a direct correlation to the results that you will achieve. From this point on, we are going to change our habits, thoughts, and internal conversation through affirmations.

Take a few minutes and write down five thoughts you tell yourself daily. (For example, you might say, "I am lazy," or "I constantly forget to do things.") Go ahead. I'll wait!

1._____

2._____

3._____

4._____

5._____

Now, take each of those five thoughts and change the phrasing to state the positive, creating an Affirmation. (For example, "I am learning to value key projects while balancing my life," or "I have a great system to remind myself of what I will accomplish.")

Planestorming!

1._____

2._____

3._____

4._____

5._____

Did that take some time? It's okay if it did.

And if it didn't, perhaps you need to dive in deeper. In fact, why don't you go for five more of each?

Words I use to destroy myself daily:

6._____

7._____

8._____

9._____

10._____

Affirmations alternative to my destructive thoughts:

6._____

7._____

8._____

9._____

10._____

Did that make you think deeper? I hope so! If you didn't get to ten, try to be more aware of your thought patterns in the coming days and add to your list!

Here's the bad news: These slight modifications, on their own, won't move your gauge.

Are you ready for the good news?

If you consistently speak these positive affirmations to yourself, over time they will mold you into a brand-new person. I have seen people radically change for the great by doing this exercise.

Does this feel awkward or hard? Well, this is a good day for you.

God, in His Word, has already told you who you are! So why not do as He says:

"Do not conform to the pattern of this world, but be transformed by the renewing of your mind." (Romans 12:2 NIV)

Planestorming!

Take some quiet time to read each scripture below and write what God says about you. I've given you some prompts, but feel free to go in your own direction. Let the Spirit lead you! (And oh yeah, these techniques build on each other—so don't forget the last lesson. Do you remember it? Start with prayer!)

"For we know, brothers and sisters loved by God, that he has chosen you." (1 Thessalonians 1:4 NIV)

I am_____

_____

_____

_____

"I praise you because I am fearfully and wonderfully made; your works are wonderful, I know that full well." (Psalm 139:14 NIV)

I am_____

_____

_____

_____

"Do not fear, for I have redeemed you; I have summoned you by name; you are mine." (Isaiah 43:1 NIV)

All my past sins and mistakes are _____

_____

_____

_____

_____

"Have I not commanded you? Be strong and courageous. Do not be afraid; do not be discouraged, for the Lord your God will be with you wherever you go." (Joshua 1:9 NIV)

In God's power, I am _____

_____

_____

_____

_____

"See what great love the Father has lavished on us, that we should be called children of God! And that is what we are!" (1 John 3:1 NIV)

I am covered by _____

_____

_____

_____

_____

"It is God who arms me with strength and keeps my way secure." (Psalm 18:32 NIV)

I can fly to higher elevations because _____

_____

_____

_____

_____

_____

"No, in all these things we are more than conquerors through him who loved us." (Romans 8:37 NIV)

I can overcome any strongholds because _____

_____

_____

_____

_____

"But thanks be to God! He gives us the victory through our Lord Jesus Christ." (1 Corinthians 15:57 NIV)

My future is secure because God has given me _____

_____

_____

_____

_____

"For I am convinced that neither death nor life, neither angels nor demons, neither the present nor the future, nor any powers, neither height nor depth, nor anything else in all creation, will be able to separate us from the love of God that is in Christ Jesus our Lord." (Romans 8:38-39 NIV)

I am so important to God that _____

_____

_____

_____

_____

_____

WOW! That's powerful stuff, right? Now here are a few questions to consider:

- Do you believe God?
- Do you believe what He says about you?
- Do you believe His promises to you?

I have left pages at the end of this book for you to journal further. You may want to consider stopping now and really delving into these questions.

If there is a disconnect between God's words and your thoughts, consider memorizing some of these verses and repeating them over and over to yourself. God's Word is powerful and can change the way you think.

Once you change the way you think, you will start to change the way you speak.

And once you change the way you speak, you will begin to change the way you do.

I promise you, once you change the way you do, you will change the way that you live. And it will be for the better. You will be able to complete all the wonderful goals you have never accomplished, and your life will be amazing!

Planestorming!

Safety Card

For more than just an emergency.

D o you ever read that safety card thing in your seat pocket? It looks so confusing, with lots of arrows and pictures. Hopefully, you will never have to use it; however, it can save your life. So can this chapter!

Your life safety card is your wellness plan.

What is your wellness plan? And no. Eating bonbons, sitting on your sofa, and binge-watching old shows every night doesn't count.

The safety card instructs you toward a path that leads to wellness. Following its steps may necessitate change—and change can be uncomfortable. Yet it is essential for personal growth.

Let's look at the areas we will be covering in this chapter:

1.   Upgrade your Physical health

2.   Boost your Mental health
3.   Keep It All In Check

UPGRADE YOUR PHYSICAL HEALTH

When was your last visit to the doctor for an annual physical? If it was over a year ago, schedule it ASAP! Catching illnesses early on can make a huge difference in your life.

What about the dentist? Yeah, do that too.

What else is there? Exercise! What do you like to do? Whatever it is, get back into a routine of fitting it into your schedule at least three times per week. Our physical health is the driving force that allows us to accomplish things.

As you read this, you may be thinking about the time you wasted $50-$100 a month on a gym membership that you didn't use. If that's what is stopping you from exercising, then get up 15 minutes ahead of your normal schedule TOMORROW and go for a leisurely jog.

After my wife passed, I knew that some form of exercise was mandatory for my health and mental toughness, so I joined a boxing gym. I paid for an entire year upfront. And because I do not like to waste money, this motivated me to work out a minimum of three times per week. This new routine caused me to burn calories, leading me to choose to eat a healthy diet simultaneously. The results: I lost 25 pounds and was in the best shape I had been in years!

Let me encourage you not to spend a lot of time planning this step. It's easy to get lost in the clouds thinking about how good your life can be instead of putting in the time and effort to get there. Here's a tip from an old slogan you may recognize: Just Do It! If you spend your time merely thinking, chances are you will never do it. Then the instructions on the safety card have no purpose. You CAN NOT afford to skip this critical step.

As you continue Planestorming, here's an exercise to help you achieve and maintain your optimum physical potential. Know that following these steps can save your life.

What exercises do you enjoy? (Think back to your childhood. Was swimming a hobby you loved? How about finding your groove on the dance floor? Maybe organized sports were your thing. Or what about nature walks or bike rides?)

_____

_____

_____

_____

Planestorming!

Is money a detriment to getting yourself physically fit? A helpful hint is to think about **what exercises you can start today that you already have the equipment for.** (Walking the dog is good for both you and your best friend! Weeding the garden helps get those squats in. Opt to move your body by bypassing the people movers and escalators.)

_____

_____

_____

_____

What doctors' appointments have you been remiss in scheduling? (Primary care physicians, specialists your body may require, dentists, optometrists, or even nutrition experts?)

_____

_____

_____

_____

_____

What foods are you serving yourself that would be better left on the flight attendant's cart? (Passing on foods that slow your body down or add inflammation, bloating, brain fog, and fatigue are those you should avoid. Additionally, to be in optimum shape, be aware of your specific medical conditions and how nutrition can affect you. Much of this can be addressed by your medical professional, but I suspect that through years of maintaining your own flight equipment, you are already aware of many of your body's particular nuances.)

_____

_____

_____

_____

_____

_____

_____

_____

Planestorming!

Having processed these questions, what changes are you willing to commit to in order to give yourself a smooth flight? Let's start with this question:

What three detrimental elements will you eject?

1._____

2._____

3._____

What three elements will you put in place to ascend to maximum physical health?

1._____

2._____

3._____

BOOST YOUR MENTAL HEALTH

Yeah, you need to work on that too! But how?

Sure, we all suffer from pain and hurt from the past. But we were never meant to live in that pain.

The first step is to process and unpack where you are. This can be accomplished through communication in the form of journaling or talking to a trusted friend or family member. Your best connection for this purpose (and He is available to all passengers) is the ONE we can pray to. (Remember your affirmations? God is always with you, and He is your best wingman ever.)

It may be time, however, to grab the bull by the horns, face the music, and head to a navigation specialist whose focus is to help you reach peaceful heights. This may include taking time for individual counseling, group therapy, or undergoing evaluations that may lead to massage therapy or learning new breathing or meditation techniques. I recommend all of the above.

It is necessary that we consistently schedule time for our mental health care. Please don't gossip with your BFF for 3 hours and think this is what it takes. Your BFF can be a great place to start, but to be truly effective, you must intentionally address and narrow down the key issues that affect your life. Sometimes we need to set a plan to fly directly through a storm so we can reach healthier and happier heights. This process, though turbulent, will lead to growth, maturity, and progress.

Here are some steps to help you keep your mental wellness intact.

Planestorming!

Consider: *What daily moments of relief can you incorporate into your life?*

_____

_____

_____

_____

_____

_____

_____

_____

_____

_____

Let's broaden that scope!

What weekly activity will motivate you into a productive schedule?

_____

_____

_____

_____

Don't stop there! Dream a little!

What motivating activity can you look forward to in the next year?

_____

_____

_____

_____

KEEP IT ALL IN CHECK

Now that you have begun this process, here is a checklist to help you get and stay on track.

____ I have completed my personal physical health evaluation and recognize what issues I need to address.

____ I have put an exercise plan in place.

____ Yes! All my doctor appointments are up to date.

____ I have evaluated where I am mentally—both the highs and lows of my current season.

____ I have a plan to fuel my mental health daily.

____ I have a plan to engage in a weekly recharge.

____ I am dreaming about and planning a mental fun day in the upcoming year to keep my motivation high.

Now that you have your itinerary set, don't forget to check your progress weekly. In fact, doing so daily is even better at first, so you don't lose a whole week pushing your stuff off.

As you up your game, keep tabs on your progress, making sure that you are completely HONEST with yourself. For example: Did you confront the hardest issues? Did you really give that workout all that you had? Did you do it 3x, 4x, or even 7x a week? Are you making sure your "fun" isn't turning into a checklist of its own that can lead to additional stress in your life?

The more you do (without overdoing), the better you will feel—and I guarantee that you will see a shift towards a better you. Others will also see this, and it will even become contagious among your friends and family members. If you have children, they, too, will get excited and motivated to fly higher in their own lives. It's so much easier to show someone versus just telling them, right?

Are you ready?

Start NOW!

Planestorming!

High Altitude

Realizing your spiritual growth.

W e're almost done with this new journey. Hang in there - this is the most important part of this book.

Let me just ask you directly: How is your spiritual life, and what steps are you taking to work on it?

The months after my wife passed were some of the most challenging times for my kids and me. Still, that season would have been significantly worse if my family had not built a solid spiritual foundation leading up to this point. I am so grateful to have a higher power who I know loves me and has a plan for everything and everyone. Since He created us, we should be at peace knowing He is in control.

You may have to conquer a learning curve as you travel to this place of spiritual wellness in your own life. Let me give you a little breathing room, however, as you think about this. I'm not asking you to become a spiritual giant overnight. Everyone moves at their own spiritual pace. The key word is "move" though, so no matter where you are spiritually, let me ask: Are you ready to take the next right step toward a solid future?

Let me give you some examples and a direction guide.

I. ESTABLISH YOUR BELIEFS

Think back: *Where have you seen the impossible happen in your life?* Perhaps a storm dissipated unexpectedly? Or maybe it didn't, forcing you to go through it, but you still somehow felt peace?

_____

_____

_____

_____

_____

Now that you have that in your mind, let me propose that SOMEONE actually provided for you during that period! See, the God of the Bible, who created us for His pleasure, works in our lives every day. Sometimes our belief in Him can begin simply by recognizing all He does for us each day and every season.

II. TAKE ACTION

Take that mustard-seed-sized faith, the part of you that now recognizes God exists, and take action to get to know Him better. Let me suggest a few ideas that may help.

Talk to God through prayer.

The God who created you wants to communicate with you!! That's all that prayer is. You can (and should!) hang out with Him daily. Tell Him your obstacles and share your successes. He wants to know it all—directly from your lips. Go ahead! Tell Him what's on your mind. Practice writing it below and then read it out loud to Him. That's called prayer!

Dear God.

_____

_____

_____

_____

_____

_____

_____. *Amen.*

The second way to take action is to let God talk to you through the Bible.

This can sound daunting if you've never opened the Bible, but don't be afraid! Start with an easy-to-read version (such as the New Living Translation) and begin with the Gospel of John, which tells of Jesus' life on earth and provides great examples of living an abundant life. As you read, ask God to tell you what He wants you to know today.

In fact, how about starting now!

John 3:16 (NLT) says: "For this is how God loved the world: He gave his one and only Son, so that everyone who believes in him will not perish but have eternal life."

Now ask yourself: What did God do for you?

_____

_____

Why did He do it?

_____

_____

What is the purpose of His action?

_____

_____

What does this mean?

_____

_____

Look at that! You did a Bible study!

Planestorming!

The third way you can take action is to find a place to grow.

Community is important. Finding a place where you can worship God with others and be led by a spiritual shepherd will help you soar into your future. It's important to know we have a place to go when we're having a tough time or facing a major challenge or crisis.

As you search, pray and ask God to lead you to His chosen congregation for you. Please make sure the church you attend is Bible-based and recognizes Jesus Christ as our Savior, God as our sovereign Judge, and the Holy Spirit as our Comforter and Guide. Be patient! Every church has its own culture, and it may take some time to find the one that is the answer to your prayer. You may have to try a few places. That's okay! Just schedule the time and START NOW!

So when are you going to start?

This is a good time to insert an affirmation: "I WILL START / REKINDLE MY SPIRITUAL JOURNEY NOW"!

Finally, you can take action by leading someone else.

Once you are grounded in a congregation to call home, it's your turn to help others.

Parents, I'm not just talking about your kids. I'm referring to your peers, friends, co-workers, and neighbors. People are hurt and broken, and they need others to guide them. Because of the time, talent, and treasure I have invested, I have had the opportunity to see others grow.

Over the past handful of years, I have enjoyed becoming active in a men's group with some business associates. We retreat annually, and I host a fireside chat open meeting every Sunday night at my house when I am in town. It's a forum where we can discuss issues and challenges and face our fears corporately. My wife also found her place. She was on the leadership team for the women's group. We saw people's lives change because they had a place to get better and draw closer to God.

"So where do I go from here?" you may be asking.

I think it's time for another checklist!

_____ I have begun a pattern of recognizing and thanking God daily with a heart of gratitude for all that He does for me.

_____ I have a scheduled time daily and weekly (at a minimum) when I dedicate my life to your higher power. (Perhaps you want to do this immediately when you wake up. Hey, you were given another day, right? Isn't that a good time to thank and praise him?)

_____ I have dedicated myself to reading and contemplating Scripture regularly—even if it is only five minutes a day.

Planestorming!

____ I did it! I found a church home and committed to attending regularly.

____ I have found a way to support others using the gifts God has given me.

Awesome job! I am very proud of how far you've come! I promise that your breakthrough is in sight and you will have a new lease on life soon!

The Cockpit

Time to map it out.

"And the LORD answered me, and said, Write the vision, and make it plain upon tables, that he may run that readeth it."
Habakkuk 2:2 KJV

At this point, you should be feeling really, really good about the progress you have made. You should be very proud of yourself. It is doubtful that you are at this point the same day you started this book. At the same time, hopefully, it has not been a year or longer since you began.

Your landing gear is up, but you are not yet at maximum cruising speed. So, where do we go from here?

Planestorming!

In order for your goals to manifest, you must actually do the work three times.

Yes, I said three times!

No, you don't have to go to the gym three times in one day. And you don't have to attend your religious service of choice morning, noon, and night. (However, if you did both of those at that pace, you would probably feel amazing.)

You are now in the cockpit and ready to map out your course.

Even though we are in a world of GPS and high-image satellites, a great pilot will still spend time strategizing their flight path. So, you need to do the same thing.

First, you need to envision your goals in your mind. We will spend more time on the actual goals in the next chapter. But for now, I'm referring to taking the time to think about what you want and how you want to live the rest of the years you have on earth.

I hope your end goal is not riding the 7:30 AM commuter train and trekking through slush only to arrive 2 minutes late to your dead-end job and be chewed out by your boss, who tells you when you can go potty!

Now I do understand you may have a family to feed, or maybe you are young and need to go through the steps society tells you and get the necessary experience until you feel you can branch out on your own. So I'm not telling you to fire your boss yet!

But I am asking that you find some time to pause and really think about the near future.

Go ahead, pause right now. Take a deep breath, forget about your worries, and think. Spend a few minutes just listening to the thoughts running through your mind.

What do you see yourself doing for a profession?

_____

_____

_____

_____

What do you DREAM about doing for a profession?

_____

_____

_____

_____

_____

_____

Where do you want to live?

_____

_____

_____

What does your family situation look like and how does that play into your future?

_____

_____

_____

_____

_____

_____

_____

_____

_____

When will you retire? WHERE will you retire?

_____

_____

_____

_____

_____

Great job. You have completed the first step of this section. I suggest you come back here often and do this again before life passes you by! Now it's time to discuss the next step.

Planestorming!

Next, you need to write down your goals.

In Habakkuk, God gave the instructions to write the vision He provided on tablets.

Pretty amazing how the prophets of yesteryear knew about the forthcoming technology! Just kidding, tablets in ancient times were large pieces of slate.

So it's time to grab your chisel and rock! Okay, not really. You can use a pen and paper or the electronic device of choice for this part.

This is the time when you document everything with regard to your goals. This is the time to Planestorm! Of course, you don't have to be on a plane to do this part. Personally, I have had much success mapping out my goals while I am traveling via airplane. However, don't wait until your next flight. We must keep the momentum and start this process ASAP.

So decide on your means of recording and plan to be structured. This document will become fuel for your growth, enabling you to reach Mach speed. This is where you will jot down everything that comes to your mind. I want you to dream and soul search.

Think of this as a there's-no-reach-too-high session. Nothing is unattainable or unachievable! Let your thoughts soar.

Write whatever comes into your mind. This could be anything, but it must be what you want or desire instead of what you think your parents or kids or society want for you. This is a safe place where you can put ink to paper or button to pixel what you envision for YOUR LIFE!

Enjoy! Dream! Think BIG! Go ahead, take a few minutes and do a quick trial run. You will need to spend way more than 2 minutes, but consider this to be a practice session. This is a time to put your head IN the clouds!

_____

_____

_____

_____

_____

_____

_____

_____

_____

_____

_____

_____

_____

_____

_____

_____

_____

_____

_____

Awesome job! Let me encourage you to return to this. The more you dream, the higher you'll fly!

Now it's time for step three.

Are you ready? For this action, you will need to rely on Steps 1 and 2. So make sure you ascend from the ground and allow the jet stream to carry you. Don't fight the momentum!

First, look back at Steps 1 and 2 through the lens of possibility and determination. Although your dreams may seem super scary, trust that you have been prepared for this moment. I know that you can do it.

If you are feeling overwhelmed, let me encourage you to start with three goals. Then, dream about practical steps you can take to achieve each of these goals. For example, if you said you want to live by the beach, brainstorm a pathway that might land you in the sand! I've written out an example and given you a template to work in on the following pages.

Planestorming!

GOAL: Live by the beach so I can build sand castles on Saturdays.

POSSIBLE STEPS TO REACH MY GOAL:

- Research companies in my field that are near the beach.
- Reach out to those companies and set up informational interviews so I can flaunt my stuff.
- Explore what qualifications I may be missing that will help me get hired.
- Sign up for an online class to gain the necessary skills.
- Start a side hustle or Plan B (that could become Plan A!) and save/invest the proceeds so you can relocate.

Do you get the idea? Every dream is achievable if you break it down into bite-sized pieces with actionable goals. It's your turn!

GOAL: _____

POSSIBLE STEPS TO REACH MY GOAL:

_____

_____

_____

_____

_____

_____

_____

_____

_____

_____

_____

GOAL: _____

POSSIBLE STEPS TO REACH MY GOAL:

_____

_____

_____

_____

_____

_____

_____

_____

_____

_____

_____

_____

GOAL: _____

POSSIBLE STEPS TO REACH MY GOAL:

_____

_____

_____

_____

_____

_____

_____

_____

_____

_____

GOAL: _____

POSSIBLE STEPS TO REACH MY GOAL:

_____

_____

_____

_____

_____

_____

_____

_____

_____

_____

_____

Now, set a time weekly to monitor your plan. Develop a pace that is conducive to your lifestyle. Eventually, you will get into a rhythm and will become a master vision achiever. The going may be turbulent at times, but you will look back and be so grateful that you went the distance. Just remember, the more you hold yourself accountable and the faster pace you travel, the sooner you will reach your dream destination.

Even if you don't achieve everything, do not be too hard on yourself. Just keep trying and celebrate small victories. You are doing fantastic work and are on a fast course to success!

I know you can do it! And I cannot wait to hear the testimonies from you.

Planestorming!

Time to Taxi

Rolling into your final destination.

Okay, you are doing great. You know what you have to do. And I think you understand why you have to do it.

Now you have to figure out what you are aiming for in life. What are your ultimate goals? Goals are very very important; they determine our initial and final approach. You may ask, "What kind of goals do I need?"

The answer to that question is as limitless as the sky. Your goals can be hourly, daily, weekly, monthly, annual, or even lifetime goals.

Perhaps you might be saying, "I don't know where to start."

Let me assure you that is perfectly normal. And that is also the reason why most people do not have goals. Instead, they just wake up, get dressed, go to their jobs and follow instructions, eat a few times, come home, go to bed, and do it all over again. Sound familiar?

But if you are this far in the book, that is who you USED TO BE! Now we will work on who you will BECOME! I know. It's both exciting and nerve-wracking at the same time. Remember, don't overthink— just do the work one knot at a time.

You have already completed one of the hardest parts: dreaming up your goals and putting them on paper. Perhaps you've even made some headway as you've applied the exercises I've shared. Now it's time to chart your progress.

CHARTING YOUR COURSE

An essential part of a safe descent is following the prescribed steps, from holding the yoke steady to correctly lowering the landing gear. Still, each step is carefully orchestrated based on the specific flight conditions and flight pattern, so your landing may look different than mine.

The important thing at this point is to categorize what you have discovered in the previous chapters and consolidate this information onto one piece of paper. When Christine and I were in the early stages of building our business, our business mentor taught us to have a sheet of paper that we would prepare each December. It had to be completed AND laminated (I know it sounds crazy) before January 1. If I waited beyond then, it wouldn't happen, and my goals for the year usually did not manifest. Trust me, taking this step will launch you immediately into action mode.

So if today is February 13, make your goals from February 14 through December 31, then you can do your full-year goals and resume on the same cycle as the annual calendar.

"How do I do it?" you might ask.

Here is one idea: On your paper, create a column on the left and write each month of the year. Then, across the top, write a title for each goal you want to achieve (i.e., your diet or exercise regimen). Next, determine an achievable and measurable goal for each category each month. For example, under "Exercise," you could write the number of times you want to go to the gym.

Got the idea? Now it's your turn! You can use the blank form on page 79 or make your own version. Perhaps you want to make one for each week or for each month. Please feel free to email me if I can send you a form. (I'm not going to create one of those self-promoted web pages so you can go on it and spend more $. Lol.)

Planestorming!

My advice is that you be as realistic as possible. Make sure that you are conscious of your schedule and factor in some time to take a break. Remember, you might have a vacation or two planned. Be mindful: a vacation is a break from the routine. Don't go too crazy, but we all need to take time to smell the flowers!

Max Gold

	Family	Worship	Work	Fitness
Jan				
Feb				
Mar				
Apr				
May				
June				
July				
Aug				
Sept				
Oct				
Nov				
Dec				

SET YOUR REWARDS

You aren't done yet! You've charted your intended progress, now, on the back side of your laminated sheet, let's set your rewards.

When I was training to compete in a half-triathlon, Coach Hector advised me not to consume more food than I needed, even after a hard workout. He said I'm not a dog that needs a reward after going to the bathroom. Mean!

However, it did make me think before eating those cookies in our cookie jar! Somehow, I had this feeling of entitlement. Because I was burning a ton of calories, it seemed okay to eat cookies—and even cheeseburgers and whatever else I wanted daily! And although I didn't gain any weight while training, I didn't lose any, either!

It can be tempting to overindulge in the good life, thinking we deserve it. Striking a balance between our work and our rewards helps us realize the benefits of our accomplishments. Putting a reward system in place can help us do just that. That's what the back of your page is for!

The first thing you need to do for this to work is make your rewards correspond to your goals.

For example, if you went to the gym two times a week for a month, should you reward yourself? That is a trick question! What was your goal that particular month? If you had planned on working out three times a week, then maybe you need to work to get back in the saddle. But if you knew you had a particularly packed month of work and you still stretched and set a goal of working out two times a week, and you did, then it is time for a celebration.

Now let's talk about the rewards you might offer yourself. Most people are not money motivated, so think beyond that. I have worked with thousands of people in my career; the truth is that people work for a check so they can pay their bills. That's it! (Of course, there are those outliers who are chasing dollars so they can buy yachts and sports cars.) Aren't we more impressed when a professional athlete receives a medal or championship trophy than when he signs his multimillion contract?

People love to hit their goals, and the idea of a reward goes beyond satisfaction with money or a material item. A reward is often a symbol of success: a T-shirt, medal, trophy, or ring we can use to show others we hit our goal and rose to the top above everyone else. Understanding this idea is extremely important for your goal and reward sheet because this applies to you too. Yes, it does!

The good news is that it probably will not cost you a lot to reward yourself when you hit your monthly goals. Maybe your reward is a "cheat meal" or a night out. Or maybe it is a symbolic, small-ticket item. Or perhaps it's some time with friends, a day trip at the beach, or a special cigar. Do you get the point?

Planestorming!

What's most important is that your reward is something you would fight for. Something that would motivate you—get you to do the work to reach your goal, especially when you do not feel like doing it. Below is an example of the reward side of your goal sheet. My best advice is not to rush the process of constructing your reward system. Take your time! Really think and pray about the things you want to achieve and the celebration you will most enjoy WHEN you accomplish your goals.

And one more thing. This is a contract with yourself! So don't forget to sign it!

WHEN I REACH MY GOAL OF _____

MY REWARD WILL BE_____

Signature: _____

You are almost done!

After you taxi, you still have to walk to another section of the airport. This one is very exclusive and reserved for you. It is in an area of the airport where very few go in life.

Are you excited?

I am excited for you! Finish this section and complete your goal card, and then I will unlock the cabin door so we can begin our journey!

Planestorming!

Private Charter

Living your dreams.

Your dreams follow your goals like a shark or hungry sea creature in the water trailing a fishing line in a moving boat.

Ever done that, by the way? You put that line in the water, and the boat kind of hums along. Seconds turn into minutes which, sometimes, turn into hours. As technology has advanced, we often want to ask the captain to just lead us right to the school for an easy catch, right?

Unfortunately, life doesn't work that way.

Most people think it does; they just play the lottery, hoping that a quick victory will change everything. The odds are so stacked against this.

We see this in professional sports too. While growing up, how many of us thought we could make it in professional sports? I was a great flag football player in and after college. I was confident that I could get a chance to walk on to a pro team or at least have a strong shot of success vs. looking like a character in Invincible when the Eagles had open tryouts. Lol! (Look up and watch the clip when time permits.)

Anyway, thousands, if not millions, of actual professional athletes who do make it on teams still find their odds of success slim. That is simply not how life works. In life, we must constantly put our hand on the plow for years and, in many cases, for decades before we hit our dream life. Understand this! Accept this! Don't lollygag! Get started now! Use your goals to help you get a day closer to your dreams.

Let's get the wheels turning about your dreams.

What are they? What is a typical dream day look like? How will it feel when you reach the pinnacle of what you are aiming for?

Can you imagine the inner peace? When that tension headache fades away, won't that be amazing?

Pause for a minute; close your eyes. Breathe in slowly, think about that feeling, and slowly exhale.

Now do it again until you can truly visualize it.

For me, it's financial peace. It's watching my kids achieve their goals. It's me seeing someone I have personally trained and developed become a successful entrepreneur, never inclined to have a boss again.

Wow!

Keep your eyes closed. (I caught you cheating—because you had to read this to know to re-close them!)

Breathe. Think. Feel.

Smile.

You did it!

Now practice this daily and watch how you will feel such a sense of pride and accomplishment. Use these techniques and continue to visualize yourself in that place daily (sometimes hourly, especially on those tough days).

Continue to focus on your goals and take those baby steps. Hey, it worked for Bill Gates, right? (He didn't take a day off for seven years straight.)

YOU CAN DO IT!

I AM PROUD OF YOU!

THE MOST IMPORTANT PEOPLE IN YOUR LIFE ARE PROUD OF YOU!

GOD IS PROUD OF YOU!

Launchpad Journal

Personal notes for charting your course.

T hese next pages are for you!

Remember Habakkuk 2:2? It says, **"And the LORD answered me, and said, Write the vision, and make it plain upon tables, that he may run that readeth it."** (KJV)

You have done a lot of processing and journaling as you have taken your life to new heights. But I want to encourage you to never stop ascending! Keep writing the vision and aiming to grow toward your future. If you do, God will ensure that you will not only be able to run, but He will also give you wings to fly!

*But grow in grace,
and in the knowledge
of our Lord and
Savior Jesus Christ.
To him be glory both
now and forever.
Amen.*

2 Peter 3:18 KJV

Max Gold

But ye are a chosen generation, a royal priesthood, an holy nation, a peculiar people; that ye should shew forth the praises of him who hath called you out of darkness into his marvellous light.

1 Peter 2:9 KJV

Max Gold

_____

_____

_____

_____

_____

_____

_____

_____

_____

_____

_____

_____

For this cause we also, since the day we heard it, do not cease to pray for you, and to desire that ye might be filled with the knowledge of his will in all wisdom and spiritual understanding.

Colossians 1:9 KJV

Max Gold

_____

_____

_____

_____

_____

_____

_____

_____

_____

_____

_____

_____

_____

As ye have therefore received Christ Jesus the Lord, so walk ye in him.

Colossians 2:6 KJV

Max Gold

The righteous shall flourish like the palm tree: he shall grow like a cedar in Lebanon.

Psalm 92:12 KJV

Max Gold

Meditate upon these things; give thyself wholly to them; that thy profiting may appear to all.

1 Timothy 4:15 KJV

About the Author

Max Gold is a native New Yorker and a graduate of Boston University. After living through 9/11, he and his family moved to Orlando to start a fresh life. It was there where Max started his financial service agency. The firm grew. and after living in Florida for 20 years, Max (becoming an empty nester) decided to start a new episode in life. At the time of printing, Max will be found heading west along I-10, as he felt called to move to Santa Monica, California, and expand his business. Stay connected to see what the next chapter brings: @maximilianr717

Furthermore, Max has started a project titled Fluorescent Village as an homage to his late wife, Christine. Prior to her passing, Christine urged Max to start a non-profit involving the name fluorescent. Max purchased his first full off-grid tiny home (currently under construction) and will be available for a night's stay at a friend's property in St. Cloud, Florida. The vision is to have for- and non-profit villages around the world where single mothers, survivors of trauma, and tourists can stay and learn how to live a minimalist life filled with tranquility and joy. Stay tuned for more information.

www.ingramcontent.com/pod-product-compliance
Lightning Source LLC
Chambersburg PA
CBHW071015120626
46546CB00003B/1098